I0570325

YOUR
FAITH
IN
THE
MAKING

A 30-DAY DEVOTIONAL

LUCIA M. CLABORN

ISBN Paperback 979-8-9860477-6-8
eBook 979-8-9860477-7-5

Your Faith In The Making - A 30 Day Devotional
By Lucia M. Claborn
Copyright © 2021 by Lucia M. Claborn
All rights reserved.
Published in the United States of America.
Lucia Claborn, LLC
2586 County Road 165,
Moulton, Alabama 35650
www.LuciaClaborn.com

All scriptures are taken from the Passion Translation unless
otherwise noted.

Scripture quotations marked TPT are from The Passion
Translation®. Copyright © 2017, 2018 by Passion & Fire
Ministries, Inc. Used by permission. All rights reserved.
www.ThePassionTranslation.com.

Holy Bible, New Living Translation, copyright © 1996, 2004,
2015 by Tyndale House Foundation. Used by permission of
Tyndale House Publishers, Inc., Carol Stream, Illinois 60188.
All rights reserved.

Dedication

This devotional is lovingly dedicated to you.

As you read through the pages of this devotional, my prayer is that you will renew your mind with God's Word, ponder on the thoughts, answer the questions, and receive a greater revelation that God created you to walk by faith in every area of your life regardless of what your life appears to be like right now.

God loves you and has a greater level of faith and glory for you to enjoy and experience in your life today.

Never doubt God's mighty power to work in you and accomplish all this. He will achieve infinitely more than your greatest request, your most unbelievable dream, and exceed your wildest imagination! He will outdo them all, for his miraculous power constantly energizes you. - Ephesians 3:20

Table of Contents

Acknowledgements

Creating projects such as this does not just happen by chance. There are always those behind the scenes helping to make it a reality. I would like to thank all those dear to my heart who made this book possible.

First, I would like to thank the Holy Spirit for helping me write each devotion, which I hope will inspire you and add value to your life.

Second, thank you to Judith Taylor, my editor and publisher. You are vital to making my dreams a reality, and I would not want to be on this adventure with anyone else. Thank you for doing what you do to make my projects come to life. I appreciate your kindness and affirmations in ensuring everything is part of the process.

Introduction

By living in God, love has been brought to its full expression in us so that we may fearlessly face the day of judgment, because all that Jesus now is, so are we in this world. 1 John 4:17

God created you in His image, and He has a wonderful plan for you. This plan includes enforcing Satan's defeat and walking in victory every day of your life.

Faith is not something you are striving to achieve; you already possess the measure of faith, and it is enough to enforce Satan's defeat. As a child of God, you are everything that Jesus is. Since He is seated in the place of victory at the right hand of Father God in Christ Jesus, far above all powers and principalities and wickedness in high places, that is where you are seated also.

Although you are seated in the place of victory, victory does not just automatically happen. You must build your faith with the Word of God to receive everything Jesus has already paid the price for you to enjoy while you are here on earth.

If you want to be a victorious champion, I encourage you to read through the pages of this devotional and linger with the Holy Spirit to allow Him to reveal God's heart for you and the love He has for you. Don't rush through the pages.

To build your faith, read each scripture out loud and imagine God is speaking directly to you. Add your name to the verse to make it personal as you read it. Allow the Holy Spirit to affirm to you that your faith is the key to living victoriously. Let Him guide you into strengthening your faith through each Bible verse and devotion so you can walk in victory in every area of your life.

Meditate on the scriptures, mull them over in your mind, and answer the questions with new revelations from Father God so you can increase your faith and go to the next level.

As you begin your journey through this devotional to build your faith for victory in your life, the prayer I pray for you is from Ephesians 1:17-23: *I pray that the Father of glory, the God of our Lord Jesus Christ, would impart to you the riches of the Spirit of wisdom and the Spirit of revelation to know him through your deepening intimacy with him.*

I pray that the light of God will illuminate the eyes of your imagination, flooding you with light until you experience the full revelation of the hope of his calling—that is, the wealth of God's glorious inheritances that he finds in us, his holy ones!

I pray that you will continually experience the immeasurable greatness of God's power made available to you through faith. Then your life will be an advertisement of this immense power as it works through you! This is the mighty power that was released when God raised Christ from the dead and exalted him to the place of highest honor and supreme authority in the heavenly realm! And now he is exalted as first above every ruler, authority, government, and realm of power in existence! He is gloriously enthroned over every name that is ever praised, not only in this age but in the age that is coming!

And he alone is the leader and source of everything needed in the church. God has put everything beneath the authority of Jesus Christ and has given him the highest rank above all others. And now we, his church, are his body on the earth and that which fills him who is being filled by it!

Day 1
Faith By My Works

So then faith that doesn't involve action is phony. But someone might object and say, "One person has faith and another person has works." Go ahead then and prove to me that you have faith without works and I will show you faith by my works as proof that I believe. James 2:17-18

My precious child, I have given you the measure, or My measure, of faith to accomplish everything I have put in your heart to carry out while you are living here on the earth!

You are more than able to step out with the faith you currently possess to move forward toward executing your dreams and goals, so don't limit yourself by negative thinking.

Don't just continue talking about what you want to do or what you are planning to do; rather, pull up your courage and take a step of faith. Trust Me to lead and guide you as you move into the wonderful future I have prepared for you.

Do you realize I have every day of your life already planned out for you? In your obedience to do the work I have assigned to you to fulfill; I will bless you and the work of your hands.

Your faith to act upon My promptings proves that you trust Me, and the result will be that you will live a very blessed and fruitful life.

Prayer – *Father God, thank You, that You already have every detail of every day of my life planned out for me. I am asking you in the Name of Jesus to help me realize this and be more aware that I can step out with confidence, boldness, and faith to do the works you designed me to accomplish. Thank You, Father, that my works are proof that I believe.*

Thoughts to Ponder.

When you step out in faith to do what God has told you to do, regardless of whether you feel qualified or capable to do the job, God honors your faith and blesses you. Your courage to act and move in obedience to His Word takes your faith to another level. When you realize God is always faithful to you, you become an unstoppable force to be reckoned with.

Taking Action To Grow Your Faith.

What is one thing from this verse that God is affirming to you right now regarding faith?

_____

_____

_____

After meditating on this verse, how does it inspire you to re-evaluate your faith journey?

_____

_____

_____

How will you apply this verse to your life so you can begin walking in even more faith to rise to a higher level of victory in your life?

_____

_____

_____

Day 2
Jesus Birthed Faith Within You

We look away from the natural realm and we focus our attention and expectation onto Jesus who birthed faith within us and who leads us forward into faith's perfection. His example is this: Because his heart was focused on the joy of knowing that you would be his, he endured the agony of the cross and conquered its humiliation, and now sits exalted at the right hand of the throne of God!
Hebrews 12:2

My beloved child, are you constantly looking at the events taking place around the world or what is happening in your life and the lives of those you love?

By setting your attention on the things of this world, you suffer much anxiety, distress, and discouragement.

I have the solution to help you overcome this world and walk in even greater levels of peace and victory in your life. This is it: Simply turn your focus and attention away from the world and put it onto Jesus.

He will lead you forward into faith by His example. As you look at His illustration of setting His heart to focus on the joy of knowing you would be His, this helped Him endure great pain, agony, and humiliation as He endured death on the cross.

Since Jesus rose from the dead and is seated at My right hand, as My child, you are raised and seated with Him in the place of victory. Use your faith to see yourself always winning.

Prayer – *Lord Jesus, thank You for being my example of how to use my faith. Father, I am asking You to help me look away from the natural realm and focus my attention and expectation on Jesus as He leads me forward into faith's perfection. Please help me keep my focus on the answer, Your promise, and not on my situation or circumstances.*

Thoughts to Ponder.

Jesus is your example of faith. Instead of staying with God and the angels in Heaven's Glory, His love for you enabled Him to choose to come to earth and die a cruel death on the cross. The thought of you being with Him for eternity gave Him great joy and strength to endure the cross, putting His trust and faith in His Father, God, to raise Him from the dead on the third day.

Taking Action To Grow Your Faith.

What is one thing from this verse that God is affirming to you right now regarding faith?

_____

_____

_____

After meditating on this verse, how does it inspire you to re-evaluate your faith journey?

_____

_____

_____

How will you apply this verse to your life so you can begin walking in even more faith to rise to a higher level of victory in your life?

_____

_____

_____

Day 3
Empowered To Live By Faith

This gospel unveils a continual revelation of God's righteousness – a perfect righteousness given to us when we believe. And it moves us from receiving life through faith, to the power of living by faith. This is what the Scripture means when it says: "We are right with God through life-giving faith!" Romans 1:17

My dearest child, I made you righteous when you accepted My Son, Jesus, as your savior.

When you believe I rose Him from the dead and seated Him at My right hand, I count this as you are being faithful to Me.

Not only does this qualify you to receive life through using your faith, but it also moves you into the power of living your life by faith. When you live your everyday life by using your faith to receive what Jesus has already paid the price for you to receive, I consider you in right standing with Me.

As you believe My Word and stir up your faith to step out on what you believe, you move from being helpless, powerless, and unable to take effective actions into an explosive faith that is demonstrated in My Word.

Again, dear one, when you trust Me and walk by faith, you are in right standing with Me – you are righteous.

P*rayer – God, thank You for making me righteous when I chose Your Son, Jesus, to be my Lord and Savior. I am asking You, in the Name of Jesus, to give me a greater revelation of the power I walk in when I live by faith. Please forgive me when I doubt what is possible when I put my trust in You. I decree I live every day exercising my explosive, miracle-working faith.*

Thoughts to Ponder.

Your faith is what God honors as righteousness, in right standing with Him. As you activate your faith by believing in your heart and speaking what you believe, your words create power to activate God's resurrection power in your life. When you put your faith in the finished work of Jesus on the cross and appropriate that power in your life, God sees you as righteous.

Taking Action To Grow Your Faith.

What is one thing from this verse that God is affirming to you right now regarding faith?

_____

_____

_____

After meditating on this verse, how does it inspire you to re-evaluate your faith journey?

_____

_____

_____

How will you apply this verse to your life so you can begin walking in even more faith to rise to a higher level of victory in your life?

_____

_____

_____

Day 4
Your Faith Is Victorious Power

You see, every child of God overcomes the world, for our faith is the victorious power that triumphs over the world.
1 John 5:4

You are My precious child, and you are stronger than you think you are! Right now, you have access to My victorious overcoming power living inside of you! It is time to activate your faith to go to an even higher level.

Your faith is that victorious power that triumphs over every circumstance and situation you or your loved one is facing today.

I have given you the measure of faith! It is the same faith that Jesus enjoyed when He walked on this earth. However, it is your responsibility to grow your faith, stand in faith, and be fully persuaded that your faith will produce the results you desire in your life.

If you want to be a powerful, confident person in your spiritual walk and have strong, mountain-moving faith, then you must spend time with Me by reading My Word. Study and meditate on My promises because this is the only way for you to reach the level of faith you desire.

Prayer – *God, I thank You for giving me a measure of the same faith You gave Jesus. I realize I have enough faith to receive results to my prayers right where I am. However, I am asking You to give me a greater desire to study and hear Your Word on a consistent basis so I can strengthen my faith and go to an even greater level of faith so I can overcome everything in this world.*

Thoughts to Ponder.

God has already given you victory over everything in this world through the death, burial, and resurrection of Jesus Christ. As a child of God, you continuously overcome the challenges of this world by using your faith. Your faith is the victorious power that triumphs over Satan and the world every time! Your faith allows you to see your victory twice, both spiritually and physically.

Taking Action To Grow Your Faith.

What is one thing from this verse that God is affirming to you right now regarding faith?

_____

_____

_____

After meditating on this verse, how does it inspire you to re-evaluate your faith journey?

_____

_____

_____

How will you apply this verse to your life so you can begin walking in even more faith to rise to a higher level of victory in your life?

_____

_____

_____

Day 5
Faith By Trusting His Power

For God intended that your faith not be established on man's wisdom but by trusting in his almighty power.
1 Corinthians 2:5

My darling, rather than putting your faith and trust in your own wisdom or the wisdom of another person, My desire is that you would only put your trust in Me. Believe My Holy Spirit to release His mighty power in you to do marvelous exploits or to manifest what your heart desires.

A benefit of trusting Me is that I establish you in everything you do and everywhere you go. Simply put your complete trust and confidence in Me and the plans I have for your life will be established. My Holy Spirit empowers you to fulfill these plans and do even greater things than you can imagine.

Ask for My wisdom and receive it. I am liberally giving you wisdom today. As you mature even more spiritually, My wisdom will be revealed to you through greater revelations of My mysteries.

Come to Me. Spend time with Me. Let's commune together so I can reveal more of Myself and My goodness to you. As a result, you will build your faith to trust Me even more as you go through your day today.

Prayer – *Father, thank You, that You give me wisdom when I ask for it, and You do not hold anything back from me. I am asking You to give me greater revelations of Your mysteries so I can put my complete trust in You and not in another person. I am asking You to establish my faith in Your Word and the promises You have already given me, and I receive it now.*

Thoughts to Ponder.

You can ask a multitude of counselors for advice about what to do in a particular situation, and you will undoubtedly receive a multitude of answers. However, if you would always like to know exactly what to do, when, and how to do it, ask God to give you wisdom. He will give you wisdom, so you know exactly what to do, when, and how to do it. Results produce greater faith.

Taking Action To Grow Your Faith.

What is one thing from this verse that God is affirming to you right now regarding faith?

_____

_____

_____

After meditating on this verse, how does it inspire you to re-evaluate your faith journey?

_____

_____

_____

How will you apply this verse to your life so you can begin walking in even more faith to rise to a higher level of victory in your life?

_____

_____

_____

Day 6
Your Faith Is Strong

Then Jesus answered her, "Dear woman, your faith is strong! What you desire will be done for you." And at that very moment, her daughter was instantly set free from demonic torment. Matthew 15:28

My cherished child, I have given you the measure of faith. What you do with that faith is your choice. You can grow your faith to receive everything I have prepared for you before you were born, or you can choose to live a mediocre life of doubt and unbelief, resulting in you not receiving what I have created for you.

I encourage you to grow your faith by hearing My Word again and again until you have an unshakable, confident expectation of what I will do for you.

Your strong faith will lead to positive changes in your life, overflow blessings, healing, and favor in every situation. Your faith will bring days of Heaven on earth into your life.

Whatever your heart desires will be done for you if you grow your faith into strong faith to receive the blessings I have designed specifically for you.

Do not give up, give in, or back down when situations appear contrary to what I have promised you. Continue to walk in strong faith, and you will receive everything I have prepared for you.

Prayer - *Father, thank You for giving me the measure of faith. I am asking You to give me a desire to hear Your Word on a consistent basis so I can grow my faith into strong faith. I decree my faith is strong. I have unshakable faith to receive everything You have prepared for me so I can not only change my world but also the lives of the people around me.*

Thoughts to Ponder.

A non-Jewish woman, a woman with no covenant, came and bowed down before Jesus, asking Him to heal her daughter. He called her a dog and told her to go away. She was not moved by His comments. Rather, she agreed with Him and asked again. He recognized her faith and granted her request. As God's child, you have a Covenant with Him that is enforced with your faith.

Taking Action To Grow Your Faith.

What is one thing from this verse that God is affirming to you right now regarding faith?

_____

_____

_____

After meditating on this verse, how does it inspire you to re-evaluate your faith journey?

_____

_____

_____

How will you apply this verse to your life so you can begin walking in even more faith to rise to a higher level of victory in your life?

_____

_____

_____

Day 7
The Fullness Of Your Faith

Jesus replied, "Listen to the truth. If you do not doubt God's power and speak out of faith's fullness, you can also speak to a tree and it will wither away. Even more than that, you could say to this mountain, 'Be lifted up and be thrown into the sea' and it will be done. Everything you pray for with the fullness of faith you will receive!" Matthew 21:21-22

My child, you are mightier than you realize when you stand in faith and do not doubt in your heart that My power is readily available and will back you up when you speak My Words.

Your spoken words, when they are My words spoken in faith, will cause life or death to manifest in your life. Your faith-empowered words will move mountains. Mountains represent kingdoms, and you have creative power in your spoken words as well as faith's fullness in your heart to move physical creations around you when you speak to them and tell them to move or be cast into the sea.

Spiritual as well as physical creations will obey your faith-filled words when you speak to them with authority.

As a born-again believer in My Son, Jesus, your faith unlocks great authority so you can walk in victory. Everything you pray for and release your faith to receive will be yours. All things are possible when you walk in and live your life by faith.

Prayer – *Father, thank You for teaching me how to live my life by faith. Thank You that all of the spiritual and physical creations are subject to my authority. I am asking You to give me even more revelation and knowledge of the power and authority I walk in when I speak Your Words and release my faith to receive the answers to my prayers.*

Thoughts to Ponder.

The truth of what Jesus taught His disciples about living a life of faith still stands today as an example for us to experience. If you do not doubt God's power and speak out of a heart that is fully persuaded in faith, you can speak to a tree or anything else, and it will obey you just like the fig tree did when Jesus spoke to it. Everything you pray for in full faith, you will receive!

Taking Action To Grow Your Faith.

What is one thing from this verse that God is affirming to you right now regarding faith?

_____

_____

_____

After meditating on this verse, how does it inspire you to re-evaluate your faith journey?

_____

_____

_____

How will you apply this verse to your life so you can begin walking in even more faith to rise to a higher level of victory in your life?

_____

_____

_____

Day 8
Let God's Faith Be In You

Jesus replied, "Let the faith of God be in you! Listen to the truth I speak to you: Whoever says to this mountain with great faith and does not doubt, 'Mountain, be lifted up and thrown into the midst of the sea,' and believes that what he says will happen, it will be done. This is the reason I urge you to boldly believe for whatever you ask for in prayer— be convinced that you have received it and it will be yours. Mark 11:22-24

My treasured child, let My faith come alive in you and be resiliently strong and unwavering in difficult times. I am telling you the truth when I tell you that you have mountain-moving faith on the inside of you.

Whatever challenge or situation you are facing today, it is your mountain. I have given you creative power in your words to speak in faith to those contemptuous situations, and they will move.

The key is to not doubt in your heart but to boldly decree and believe that I will do what you say when you release your faith-filled words over your situation and circumstance.

My Son, Jesus, is your example of how active faith works. Whatever you ask for in prayer, you must be convinced that you receive it when you ask, and it will be yours. This is my promise to you.

Prayer – *Father God, I humble myself before you. I am asking You to strengthen my faith, so I believe I receive the answers to my prayers the moment I pray them. By faith, I decree I have mountain-moving faith, and I believe my bold, confident faith in Jesus is producing the results I want in my life. Thank You, Lord, that my faith-filled words produce a great harvest.*

Thoughts to Ponder.

As a child of God, you have access to God-like faith. Yes! You have the Godkind of faith residing inside of you. So why would you ever doubt what your faith will produce in your life? Never allow your heart to be divided or undecided about what is possible for you to accomplish or achieve in your life. Your faith will lift you up to a higher level in God's Kingdom.

Taking Action To Grow Your Faith.

What is one thing from this verse that God is affirming to you right now regarding faith?

_____

_____

_____

After meditating on this verse, how does it inspire you to re-evaluate your faith journey?

_____

_____

_____

How will you apply this verse to your life so you can begin walking in even more faith to rise to a higher level of victory in your life?

_____

_____

_____

Day 9
Live By Faith

For we live by faith, not by what we see with our eyes.
2 Corinthians 5:7

My spectacular child, how I long for you to see beyond the physical realm and what you are seeing with your natural eyes. There is so much more to your life and this world than what meets your eyes every day.

I understand that while you are living on earth, your spirit man, the real you, longs to be with Me in your Heavenly home. I encourage you to hope on because I have prepared a wonderful place for you. And, in doing so, I am confirming My promise to you by giving you My Holy Spirit as a guarantee.

So, take heart and always be full of courage, My sweet child. You can joyful and confidently expect that I have prepared a place for you. You will not be disappointed.

I urge you to continue living your life in such a way that you please Me in everything you say and do. Your faith is the key to activating a life lived to please me.

Everything in the natural realm is subject to change and aligns with the spiritual realm when you release your faith-filled words into the atmosphere.

Speak My words regarding healing and sickness will go. Speak My Words of prosperity and lack will leave. Speak My Words of life and depression will go. Speak My Word over every area of your life, and you will live in days of Heaven on earth.

Prayer – *Father, I come to You in the mighty Name of Jesus. I thank You for the measure of faith You have given me. I ask You to help me keep my eyes focused on the spiritual realm and not solely on the physical realm. I ask You to help me focus my eyes on Your Word and keep it alive in my heart so I can change my world with Your Word.*

Thoughts to Ponder.

Everything in the natural realm is subject to change and line up with God's spiritual plans as you walk in your God-given authority. When you discern something in your life is out of order according to the Word of God, you can release your faith-filled words and demand the situation to change for the better. Your faith in the Word of God activates His power in your life.

Taking Action To Grow Your Faith.

What is one thing from this verse that God is affirming to you right now regarding faith?

_____

_____

_____

After meditating on this verse, how does it inspire you to re-evaluate your faith journey?

_____

_____

_____

How will you apply this verse to your life so you can begin walking in even more faith to rise to a higher level of victory in your life?

_____

_____

_____

Day 10
Faith Brings Hopes Into Reality

Now faith brings our hopes into reality and becomes the foundation needed to acquire the things we long for. It is all the evidence required to prove what is still unseen.
Hebrews 11:1

I call you My faithful child. Continue standing in your level of faith. Do not give up on your hopes and dreams. Your hope is what your faith attaches itself to, so your desires will become a reality!

Your faith will produce a great harvest in your life if you do not throw in the towel. You will be commended for standing in faith when you have nothing else to stand upon!

Do you realize your faith empowers you to see what your words will create before it is a reality? It does not matter what level of faith you think you are standing in; faith is faith. You have the same creative power available to you that I used when I spoke the world into existence.

You can use your faith, your faith-filled words, to bring the invisible realm into the natural physical realm by not doubting in your heart and only believing all things are possible.

Your faith is the title deed or the assurance that the things you hope for are divinely guaranteed by Me. Your faith is the evidence of the things you do not see but are convinced that they are a reality. I promise you that your faith comprehends as a fact what cannot be experienced by your physical senses.

Prayer – *Thank You, Father, that my faith is now bringing my hopes into reality and is the firm foundation I need to acquire the things I am longing for. I decree my faith is empowering my words to create my reality, bringing my desired world into existence. Thank You, Father, that my faith is my title deed with You, and You have divinely guaranteed my hopes.*

Thoughts to Ponder.

Your faith is the foundation to build upon for all the things you desire in life. You must use your faith to receive everything from Father God. It is your faith that produces a harvest in your life. Your faith is the powerful supernatural force that brings a manifestation of your heart's aspirations from the spiritual realm into the natural realm. Faith always produces results.

Taking Action To Grow Your Faith.

What is one thing from this verse that God is affirming to you right now regarding faith?

_____

_____

_____

After meditating on this verse, how does it inspire you to re-evaluate your faith journey?

_____

_____

_____

How will you apply this verse to your life so you can begin walking in even more faith to rise to a higher level of victory in your life?

_____

_____

_____

Day 11
God Rewards Your Faith

And without faith living within us it would be impossible to please God. For we come to God in faith knowing that he is real and that he rewards the faith of those who passionately seek him. Hebrews 11:6

My incredible child, I gave you a measure of faith when you chose My Son, Jesus, to be your Lord and Savior. Rest assured that you have enough faith right where you are to receive everything you desire from Me.

Your faith in knowing that I am real is what distinguishes you from others who do not know Me and those who do not trust Me. As you come to Me in prayer with bold, courageous faith, simply believing that I am God and that I exist is what brings Me great joy.

Your confidence in recognizing that I care about every detail of your life blesses Me. When you seek after Me in faith, I am delighted, and I honor your faith. As you acknowledge Me and walk with Me throughout your day, I am well pleased.

You cannot please Me apart from using your faith, and when you walk by faith, I count it unto you as righteousness. As you use your faith, you accomplish everything I have planned for you to do throughout your lifetime.

Prayer – *Father God, I am coming to You in faith, knowing that You are real and that You reward my faith because I am passionately seeking You. I recognize the greatness of who You are, and I decree that You are concerned about every detail of my life. I decree that I am living my everyday life by faith, and You are well pleased with me.*

Thoughts to Ponder.

Why would you want to live your life apart from the One who created you and knows every detail and plan for your life? If you want to live your life in such a way that pleases God, you must simply live your everyday walking around life by faith. You must believe God is real, that He exists, and you must believe He rewards you because you earnestly seek after Him.

Taking Action To Grow Your Faith.

What is one thing from this verse that God is affirming to you right now regarding faith?

_____

_____

_____

After meditating on this verse, how does it inspire you to re-evaluate your faith journey?

_____

_____

_____

How will you apply this verse to your life so you can begin walking in even more faith to rise to a higher level of victory in your life?

_____

_____

_____

Day 12

Faith Responds To God's Word

Faith, then, is birthed in a heart that responds to God's anointed utterance of the Anointed One. Romans 10:17

My celebrated child, the message of My Son, Jesus, is always near you. The word of faith is in your ears and on your lips. I sent Jesus to earth for a specific purpose, and He fulfilled that purpose.

I sent Him to fulfill the Law which He did when He died on the cross, was buried, and rose to life again on the third day. He is the end of you keeping the Law to be righteous.

When you confess that Jesus is Lord and believe in your heart that I raised Him from the dead, you are saved. You believe with your heart that you are saved, which leads to righteousness, and with your mouth, you confess Jesus as Lord, which leads to salvation.

This act of faith in receiving my Son Jesus as your Lord makes you in right standing with Me. When you believe in and trust Him, you will not be disgraced or put to shame.

My desire is that you would share the good news of My Son, Jesus, with the world so they can hear the life-changing message of salvation and call on His Name to be saved.

Faith will come to them by hearing what is told, and what is heard comes by the preaching of the message that came from the lips of Jesus, the Messiah Himself.

P**rayer** – *Father, I come boldly to the Throne Room of Grace by the Blood of Jesus. I decree my faith is growing more and more because I believe in my heart that Jesus is Your Son, and You raised Him from the dead. I am trusting in and relying on Jesus's words. Thank You, God, that I will never be put to shame or disappointed because Jesus is my Lord.*

Thoughts to Ponder.

Faith comes when you hear God's Word. When a preacher is sent to take God's Word to the nations, people look forward with great hope to hearing good news. Good news to the sick is they do not have to be sick anymore. Good news to the broke is they do not have to be broke anymore because Jesus redeemed them from the curse of sickness, disease, lack, and poverty.

Taking Action To Grow Your Faith.

What is one thing from this verse that God is affirming to you right now regarding faith?

_____

_____

_____

After meditating on this verse, how does it inspire you to re-evaluate your faith journey?

_____

_____

_____

How will you apply this verse to your life so you can begin walking in even more faith to rise to a higher level of victory in your life?

_____

_____

_____

Day 13
Complete Confidence In Jesus

This perfectly wise plan was destined from eternal ages and fulfilled completely in our Lord Jesus Christ, so that now we have boldness through him, and free access as kings before the Father because of our complete confidence in Christ's faithfulness. Ephesians 3:11-12

My dearly esteemed child, I have a perfectly wise plan established for you so you can feel confident in coming to Me with your intimate conversations, wants, needs, and desires. I created this plan before the foundation of the world, and Jesus fulfilled the plan when He was born into the earth.

Through His selfless decision to be willing, faithful, and loyal to fulfill the assignment I gave Him before He walked on the earth, you can now be certain to know that you have free access to come to Me as a king would come to Me.

You can come before Me with great boldness and with complete confidence in the finished work of My Son, Jesus. He paid the ultimate price for you to have an intimate relationship with Me.

Because of Jesus's faithfulness, you can be assured that you have the freedom of speech to say with great boldness whatever is in your heart. When you come to Me in this posture, I hear you. I am your loving Father who created you and only wants the very best of everything for your life.

Prayer – *Father, thank You for creating a wise plan from the beginning of time for me to have a relationship with You. Thank You that I can come before You with great boldness and confidence because of Jesus's faithfulness. Thank You that I have the freedom to come to You as a king would come before You to share my most intimate thoughts and heart's desires.*

Thoughts to Ponder.

God's plan from the foundation of time was for all of humanity to experience salvation through Jesus Christ. He longs to have an intimate relationship with you, so He sent Jesus to fulfill His plan to redeem you from Satan's plan. Because of your faith in Jesus, you can have the courage and confidence to approach God unreserved with freedom and without fear.

Taking Action To Grow Your Faith.

What is one thing from this verse that God is affirming to you right now regarding faith?

_____

_____

_____

After meditating on this verse, how does it inspire you to re-evaluate your faith journey?

_____

_____

_____

How will you apply this verse to your life so you can begin walking in even more faith to rise to a higher level of victory in your life?

_____

_____

_____

Day 14
You Will Do Greater Miracles

I tell you this timeless truth: The person who follows me in faith, believing in me, will do the same mighty miracles that I do—even greater miracles than these because I go to be with my Father! John 14:12

My dear child, I am telling you an eternal truth. When you follow Jesus in faith - you put your faith in Jesus - you will perform the same mighty miracles that He did when He walked the earth. Actually, you will do even greater miracles than Jesus did because He is now with Me.

Be reminded that the words Jesus spoke during His three years of earthly ministry were not His own. His words were My words because I lived in Him and performed My miracles of power through Him. He lived as one with Me, so you can have the confidence to know that I was the one doing the signs, wonders, and miracles through Him.

Because Jesus is raised and seated at My right hand in the place of victory and authority, you can be certain that I will do whatever you ask Me to do when you ask in My Son's Name. This is how Jesus will show the world what I am really like, and this brings great glory to Me.

Ask Me anything in Jesus's Name, and I will do it for you so that you will give Me the glory for the greater works I will do for you.

Prayer – *Father God, I come to You in the Name of Jesus, and I thank You for being my loving Father. Please help me realize that You are always with me to accomplish the greater miracles I ask You to do. I am using my faith to believe that You will use me as an instrument of Your love and power on earth so You can be glorified in everything I do.*

Thoughts to Ponder.

As a child of God, the fullness of the Godhead bodily lives in you. God the Father, God the Son (Jesus), and God the Holy Spirit reside in you. If you are unwavering in your belief in this power that inhabits you, you will do the same and even greater things than Jesus did, as you release your faith and trust God to do what He says He will do when you speak His Word.

Taking Action To Grow Your Faith.

What is one thing from this verse that God is affirming to you right now regarding faith?

_____

_____

_____

After meditating on this verse, how does it inspire you to re-evaluate your faith journey?

_____

_____

_____

How will you apply this verse to your life so you can begin walking in even more faith to rise to a higher level of victory in your life?

_____

_____

_____

Day 15
You Are Righteous Through Faith

So our conclusion is this: God's wonderful declaration that we are righteous in His eyes can only come when we put our faith in Christ, and not in keeping the law. Romans 3:28

My magnificent child, you are the one I made righteous when you put your faith in My Son, Jesus, My Anointed One.

As you realize everything that the Law says is addressed to those who are under its authority, so every excuse is silenced, and no one will boast that they are innocent before Me. This is so the world will be held accountable to My standards. For those who insist on observing the Law, no one earns the status of being declared righteous before Me, for it is the Law that fully empowers, exposes, and unmasks the reality of sin.

However, as My child, you are independent of the Law. My righteousness is tangible and brought to light for you through Jesus. It is My righteousness made visible through the faithfulness of Jesus to all who believe in Him that will receive the Gift of Righteousness.

It is through your faith in My Son's powerful act of redemption and forgiveness that I freely give My righteousness to you. My Gift of Love and favor is yours, all because Jesus has liberated you from the guilt, punishment, and power of sin!

Prayer – *Father God, thank You for sending your Son Jesus to fulfill the Law and the Prophets. I thank You that I am redeemed from the Law because it only empowers sin. I decree, according to Your Word, that it is my faith in Jesus, the Anointed One, that makes me righteous in Your eyes and in right standing with You.*

Thoughts to Ponder.

God already sees you as righteous, in right standing with Him. He made you in right standing with Him when you accepted Jesus as your Lord and Savior. In the Old Covenant, the Law was sent to define, restrain sin, and prove people needed God's help. In the New Covenant, where you live, being put under the Law only empowers more sin. Jesus came to fulfill the Law.

Taking Action To Grow Your Faith.

What is one thing from this verse that God is affirming to you right now regarding faith?

_____

_____

_____

After meditating on this verse, how does it inspire you to re-evaluate your faith journey?

_____

_____

_____

How will you apply this verse to your life so you can begin walking in even more faith to rise to a higher level of victory in your life?

_____

_____

_____

Day 16
God Is Faithful To His Promises

So now wrap your heart tightly around the hope that lives within us, knowing that God always keeps his promises!
Hebrews 10:23

My sweet child, because you are My child, the Blood of Jesus welcomes you to come boldly and without hesitation into My most Holy Sanctuary in the Heavenly realm.

Jesus created a new, life-giving way for you to approach Me. The veil was torn in two, giving you free and fresh access to Me when His body was beaten, bruised, and pierced.

Are you aware that you now have a magnificent High Priest in Jesus to welcome you into My house? You can approach Me with absolute trust and confidence in My power, wisdom, and goodness toward you.

You can come fully convinced that nothing will keep you at a distance from Me because your heart has been sprinkled with the Blood of Jesus to remove all impurities of guilt and shame. You are free from an accusing conscience since you are now clean, unstained, and presentable to Me both inside and out.

Wrap your heart tightly around the hope that lives within you because you can be confident that I am always reliable and faithful in keeping My promises to you.

Prayer – *Father, thank You for the Blood of Jesus, which tore the veil giving me free access to Your Holy Sanctuary. Thank You that nothing keeps me at a distance from You. Thank You for giving me even more revelation so that I can confidently put my trust in You because You are always reliable and faithful to keep Your promises to me.*

Thoughts to Ponder.

Jesus paid the price you could not pay to have the opportunity to have an intimate relationship with Father God. His shed Blood opened the door for you to have full freedom and confidence to enter into the Holy of Holies with a true, honest, and sincere heart that is purified from a guilty conscience. Therefore, you can hold onto your hope without wavering.

Taking Action To Grow Your Faith.

What is one thing from this verse that God is affirming to you right now regarding faith?

_____

_____

_____

After meditating on this verse, how does it inspire you to re-evaluate your faith journey?

_____

_____

_____

How will you apply this verse to your life so you can begin walking in even more faith to rise to a higher level of victory in your life?

_____

_____

_____

Day 17
The Lord Is For You

Those who first heard the good news of deliverance failed to enter into that realm of faith's rest because of their unbelieving hearts. Yet the fact remains that we still have the opportunity to enter into the faith-rest life and experience the fulfillment of the promise! Hebrews 4:6

My brilliant child, My desire is for you to enter into the position of faith-rest today because you believe, and you put your whole-hearted faith in My promises to you.

When you hear the Good News of deliverance as the Israelites did, or you hear any of My promises that you can appropriate into your life today, and you do not join your faith with that promise, it will not produce the fulfillment of the promise in your life.

I desire that you put your confident, unwavering faith in all of My covenant promises without doubting. I encourage you to be extremely diligent to ensure that you embrace the fullness of My promises, so you do not fail to experience them.

One of My greatest hopes is that you will confidently believe in your heart and put your complete faith into receiving what I have already prepared for you. When your faith activates My promises in your life, then you will experience the glorious realm of My confident rest!

Prayer – *Father, thank You for giving me the promise of victory in every area of my life from the foundation of the world. You are always right on time in delivering. I decree I have a believing heart and am adding my faith to receive your promises. I am entering into a faith-rest life today because I believe I receive all of Your promises. They are yes and amen.*

Thoughts to Ponder.

God's promise of entering His rest by faith is still offered to you today. You can trust Him to be right on time. He is not coming too late, nor will He be short in reaching you at the perfect time. He set a definite date and time called 'today' to give you another opportunity to enter into His faith-rest because you hear His voice, and you trust and obey His utterances.

Taking Action To Grow Your Faith.

What is one thing from this verse that God is affirming to you right now regarding faith?

_____

_____

_____

After meditating on this verse, how does it inspire you to re-evaluate your faith journey?

_____

_____

_____

How will you apply this verse to your life so you can begin walking in even more faith to rise to a higher level of victory in your life?

_____

_____

_____

Day 18
Faith Proves What Is Possible

Jesus responded, "What appears humanly impossible is more than possible with God. For God can do what man cannot." Luke 18:27

My exceptional child, what challenge or struggle are you facing today? What insurmountable mountain is staring you in the face, lying to you, and telling you that you will never be able to go over it, around it, or through it?

What lie of the enemy are you believing about yourself or your relationships that makes you think you cannot accomplish your dreams and goals and walk in success and victory?

In the natural, your situation may look impossible. However, as My child, I have already given you the power and the measure of faith to change your situation.

We are in a Covenant relationship, and as you stir up your hope in what I can do for you, it will be the anchor upon which you attach your faith.

When you confidently expect in what I can do, you will not be disappointed. I created the universe with My words, and I gave you the same creative power to change your life with the power of your words.

Invite Me into your struggles. Use My Word, My love letter to you, to build your faith and know that all things are possible when you put your faith in Me. I will do supernaturally what you cannot do naturally.

Prayer – *Father, I come before You humbly, inviting You to come into my situation. I have done everything I know to do in the natural to make the necessary changes, to no avail. It still looks impossible to me, so I am asking You to do the impossible for me today. Thank You for moving on my behalf and making the impossible possible in my life. I give You all the glory.*

Thoughts to Ponder.

Many times in life, people quit or give up when faced with things that appear to be impossible instead of increasing their faith to believe they receive the possibilities God has prepared for them. For every temptation you face to surrender your determination to pursue your victory, God has already made a way of escape. All things are possible when you rely on God.

Taking Action To Grow Your Faith.

What is one thing from this verse that God is affirming to you right now regarding faith?

_____

_____

_____

After meditating on this verse, how does it inspire you to re-evaluate your faith journey?

_____

_____

_____

How will you apply this verse to your life so you can begin walking in even more faith to rise to a higher level of victory in your life?

_____

_____

_____

Day 19
Speak In Faith

We have the same Spirit of faith that is described in the Scriptures when it says, "First I believed, then I spoke in faith." So we also first believe then speak in faith.
2 Corinthians 4:13

My priceless child, do you see how valuable you are to Me as you live your everyday life trusting Me? Do you realize that you carry immeasurable power that I placed within you so people will see that is it My power released through your life and not yours as you speak faith-filled words?

I have put the same Spirit of Faith in you that is in My Son, Jesus. Even when it seems you are surrounded by every kind of pressure, you are not crushed because of My power within you. Although people lie about you, your own fears consume you, and you are hurting from your suffering and trauma, you can still choose to stay faithful to Me and speak words of faith because you believe My Word.

I am the Lord, and I made you in My image. Whatever I speak, it shall be performed and come to pass without delays. Because you are created in My likeness, you have the power to believe and speak the Word in faith, and I will perform it for you.

Prayer – *Father, I come before You and thank You for giving me the same spirit of faith that You gave Jesus. I decree that I have mountain-moving faith, and I believe the promises in Your Word. I decree these promises over my life in faith. I believe You will perform these promises in my life as I stand unmovable in my faith.*

Thoughts to Ponder.

God made you in His likeness with the creative power of your words to change your life and speak life over those around you. By faith, you understand that the universe was created by God's words, so everything you see is not made out of things that are visible. Therefore, whatever you ask of God, believe that you have received it with your faith, and it will be yours.

Taking Action To Grow Your Faith.

What is one thing from this verse that God is affirming to you right now regarding faith?

_____

_____

_____

After meditating on this verse, how does it inspire you to re-evaluate your faith journey?

_____

_____

_____

How will you apply this verse to your life so you can begin walking in even more faith to rise to a higher level of victory in your life?

_____

_____

_____

Day 20
Established In Your Faith

Your spiritual roots go deeply into his life as you are continually infused with strength, encouraged in every way. For you are established in the faith you have absorbed and enriched by your devotion to him! Colossians 2:7

My remarkable child, your completeness is only found in Jesus as you are totally filled with Me, and the fullness of His life overflows within you.

I am greatly delighted to see you deepening your commitment to Jesus through your steadfast faith in Him. I see you are completely leaning your entire life on Him in absolute trust and confidence in His power, wisdom, and goodness toward you.

In the same way you have received Jesus as your Lord and Savior by faith, continue your journey of faith with Him. Conduct yourself so that you become more like Him by living your life and progressing further and further into your union with Him.

Again, as you grow more spiritually mature and allow your spiritual roots to go deep into His life, you are continually being infused with His strength and being encouraged even more.

You are establishing the faith you have already acquired, and your devotion to Him is enriching you in even greater ways.

Prayer – *Father God, thank You for filling me to overflowing with the fullness of You, Your Son, Jesus, and the Holy Spirit. I humble myself before You and ask You to give me the desire of my heart which is to increase my commitment to live more like Jesus so I can reflect even more of His character in my life. I am asking You to continually strengthen and encourage me.*

Thoughts to Ponder.

Rather than following human traditions and men's ideas about this material world, consider the benefits of deepening your relationship with Jesus so your spiritual roots are strengthened even more. Focusing your efforts to gain more revelation of His faithfulness will increase and establish your faith so that it is abounding and overflowing.

Taking Action To Grow Your Faith.

What is one thing from this verse that God is affirming to you right now regarding faith?

_____

_____

_____

After meditating on this verse, how does it inspire you to re-evaluate your faith journey?

_____

_____

_____

How will you apply this verse to your life so you can begin walking in even more faith to rise to a higher level of victory in your life?

_____

_____

_____

Day 21
Your Faith-filled Requests

Don't be pulled in different directions or worried about a thing. Be saturated in prayer throughout each day, offering your faith-filled requests before God with overflowing gratitude. Tell him every detail of your life. Philippians 4:6

My extravagant child, I want to encourage you to be settled in your heart, your mind, your will, and your emotions. Spend time with Me and learn how much I love you. Learn how I care for every detail of your life and am always faithful to you.

You can choose to be cheerful, living a life overflowing with joy in every season of your life. Keep in mind to be humble and allow gentleness to be seen in all of your relationships.

Do not allow yourself to be pulled in different directions, worrying about all the things in your life that you cannot control. Do not focus on the 'maybes' and the 'what-ifs.'

Instead, saturate yourself in prayer throughout your day. Thank Me for who I am to you and for what I have done in your life. Thank Me for the goodness I have shown you.

Then make your faith-filled requests to me as you are overflowing with gratitude for who I am and what I have done and will do in your life and the lives of those you love and serve.

You can tell me every concern you have regarding your life.

Prayer – *Thank You, Lord, that You are concerned about every detail of my life, and I can talk to You about all of them. I decree I am not being pulled in different directions, and I am not worried about anything in my life. I decree I am saturating my life in prayer throughout my day. I am making my faith-filled requests known to You, and believe I receive the answers.*

Thoughts to Ponder.

Although you experience challenges, you can put your faith in a loving Heavenly Father who causes you to be stable or settled in your emotions. Your faith dispels a life once lived full of worry and being pulled in different directions. As you lavish your love on God and praise Him for who He is and what He has done for you, you can make your prayer requests known to Him.

Taking Action To Grow Your Faith.

What is one thing from this verse that God is affirming to you right now regarding faith?

_____

_____

_____

After meditating on this verse, how does it inspire you to re-evaluate your faith journey?

_____

_____

_____

How will you apply this verse to your life so you can begin walking in even more faith to rise to a higher level of victory in your life?

_____

_____

_____

Day 22

Live From God's Faith

And he also says, "My righteous ones will live from my faith. But if fear holds them back, my soul is not content with them!" Hebrews 10:38

My splendid child, you are My righteous one because you are living your every day, walking around life using My faith to overcome this world. You are not moved by fear, nor is fear holding you back from completing the assignment I have given you. Therefore, My soul takes great delight in you!

It is not your character to draw back to a life of misery to be utterly destroyed. Instead, you believe in, embrace, and put your whole trust and reliance upon Me through my Son, Jesus.

You are convinced that you possess a treasure growing in heaven because of your faith, and that treasure can never be taken away from you. This revelation causes you to overflow with My joy. I am encouraging you to persist in your bold, courageous faith because you are destined for a great reward!

My desire is that your faithfulness will reflect steadfast patience and strong endurance to fully accomplish My will for your life. Then you will receive and fully enjoy everything I have prepared for you and have promised you.

It is your faith in Jesus that preserves you so you can experience true life and My uncontainable joy.

Prayer – *Father, thank You for giving me Your faith to live my life and change my world. I decree I am not fearful about anything because I am embracing You and putting my whole trust and reliance upon You. I decree that my courageous faith, steadfast patience, and strong endurance will enable me to fulfill my assignment and receive all Your promises.*

Thoughts to Ponder.

God has given you the measure of faith. The same faith Jesus used when He fulfilled His earthly ministry. He is delighted when you use bold, courageous faith to change your world and receive all the blessings He has prepared for you. Instead of being fearful and drawing back in the face of difficult situations, He expects you to live your best life by using your faith.

Taking Action To Grow Your Faith.

What is one thing from this verse that God is affirming to you right now regarding faith?

_____

_____

_____

After meditating on this verse, how does it inspire you to re-evaluate your faith journey?

_____

_____

_____

How will you apply this verse to your life so you can begin walking in even more faith to rise to a higher level of victory in your life?

_____

_____

_____

Day 23

God Is Always Faithful To You

For all of God's promises find their "yes" of fulfillment in him. And as his "yes" and our "amen" ascend to God, we bring him glory! 2 Corinthians 1:20

My cherished child, I have made countless promises to you for every situation in life that you will face, and for every emotion you will experience. You will find them hidden in My Word.

I give you these promises to build your faith and help you know what is possible for your life if you dare to believe Me. I have not changed My original plans for you, nor have I made plans for you with deceitful motives, flip-flopping with a 'yes' and then a 'no' in the same breath.

Just as I am true to My Word, you can be certain I am trustworthy and faithful to you. I mean every Word I have written to you in my Love Letters contained within your Bible. I will confirm them in your life.

I have anointed you with My Holy Spirit to strengthen you and make you steadfast, so you will be established in your relationship with Jesus. I know that you are mine because I have stamped you with My seal of love over your heart. This is my guarantee of the fulfillment of blessings to come that I have promised you.

You will always find your 'yes' answer in My Son, Jesus. He has never been 'yes' and 'no.' He is always your Divine 'yes,' your assurance that My promises are good.

Prayer – *Lord, I come before You humbly today and thank You for every promise You have given me in Your Word. I thank You that all of Your promises to me are yes, and they are amen, or so be it. I am asking You to show me the promise I need to stand on right now for the situation I am going through so I can build my faith to receive that promise.*

Thoughts to Ponder.

Regardless of what is happening in your life right now, God has over 8,500 promises in His Word for you to choose from to build your faith so you can come out of that situation. God is not a man that He would lie to you. He has sealed you with His Holy Spirit, which is your guarantee of His promised blessings.

Taking Action To Grow Your Faith.

What is one thing from this verse that God is affirming to you right now regarding faith?

_____

_____

_____

After meditating on this verse, how does it inspire you to re-evaluate your faith journey?

_____

_____

_____

How will you apply this verse to your life so you can begin walking in even more faith to rise to a higher level of victory in your life?

_____

_____

_____

Day 24
Be Faithful To Only Believe

Jesus looked at her and said, "Didn't I tell you that if you will believe in me, you will see God unveil his power?"
John 11:40

My dearly chosen child, if I may encourage you with some wisdom, it would be that believing in My promises is the magnificent key to experiencing My glorious fingerprints on your life.

I am not a man that I would lie to you about My promises that I have given to you in My Word. When I tell you something in My Word, I will keep that promise to you. You can depend on Me, and be assured that if you walk with Me and look to Me for help, I will never fail you.

Everything is possible. What seems impossible for you will be possible if you only believe it is possible. Jesus reassured Martha that their brother would live again. Then He lifted His eyes to Me and thanked Me for hearing Him as I always did.

He prayed to Me so that those who stood with Him would believe that I sent Him to the earth as My messenger, and so they would know I gave Him the power to raise the dead.

I have placed that same resurrection power within you, and you can activate that power if you only believe it is possible.

Prayer – *Father, I come to you thanking You that You have given me the same resurrection power in my words that You gave Jesus because I believe in Jesus. Father, please show me Your promise from the Bible that I can stand on to receive what I am praying for. I am asking You to increase my faith to believe You for the seemingly impossible.*

Thoughts to Ponder.

When God created you, He made you in the image of Himself, His Son, Jesus, and His Holy Spirit. When you accepted Jesus as your Lord and Savior, He filled you with His Holy Spirit, the Spirit of Creativity. Because His Holy Spirit lives in you, there is nothing you cannot do. You have resurrection power living on the inside of you to create what you say if you will only believe.

Taking Action To Grow Your Faith.

What is one thing from this verse that God is affirming to you right now regarding faith?

_____

_____

_____

After meditating on this verse, how does it inspire you to re-evaluate your faith journey?

_____

_____

_____

How will you apply this verse to your life so you can begin walking in even more faith to rise to a higher level of victory in your life?

_____

_____

_____

Day 25
Just Keep On Believing

But Jesus refused to listen to what they were told and said to the Jewish official, "Don't yield to fear. All you need to do is to keep on believing." Mark 5:36

My fabulous child, do not listen to the negative voices in your head. Do not listen to the nay-sayers or those who would try to discourage you from believing the truths I have given you in My Word.

You may have received a bad report from the doctor, your job, or your spouse today that is contrary to the promises found in My Love Letter to you.

Do not deny the bad report; rather, choose to believe that the power found in My Word, combined with the resurrection power living inside you and released through your voice, is more than enough to change your situation.

When Jesus overheard what was being said to Jairus about his daughter's death, He ignored what they said and told him not to be seized with alarm or struck with fear. He told him to keep on believing that she would live.

When they entered the home, Jesus said to them, "Why all this grief and weeping? Don't you know the girl is not dead but merely asleep?" He tenderly clasped the child's hand in his and said to her, "Little girl, wake up from the sleep of death."

Oftentimes, things are not as they seem, and you must keep believing My promises.

Prayer – *Father God, thank You for the Blood Covenant we have with Jesus. Thank You that He paid the price with His Blood for me to walk in victory over Satan's attacks. I decree I am going to be like Jesus and refuse to listen to what others are telling me that is contrary to Your Word. I decree I will not yield to fear. I decree I will keep believing Your promises.*

Thoughts to Ponder.

Everything you need has already been provided for you through the finished work of Jesus on the cross. He was buried, went to hell, defeated Satan, and then rose again on the third day. He gave you the keys to the Kingdom and is seated at the right hand of Father God, which is the place of victory. Your responsibility is to put your faith in the finished work of Jesus and believe.

Taking Action To Grow Your Faith.

What is one thing from this verse that God is affirming to you right now regarding faith?

_____

_____

_____

After meditating on this verse, how does it inspire you to re-evaluate your faith journey?

_____

_____

_____

How will you apply this verse to your life so you can begin walking in even more faith to rise to a higher level of victory in your life?

_____

_____

_____

Day 26
Your Faith Releases Power

Jesus responded, "Beloved daughter, your faith in me released your healing. You may go with my peace."
Luke 8:48

My extraordinary child, have you suffered from sickness, disease, turmoil, distractions, or pain for many weeks, months, or years? Have you spent all you have to find the answers you are searching for, only to be left with empty pockets and the same symptoms?

Today is your day for breakthrough and turnaround. Today is your day to determine within yourself that you have spent the last day in your current situation.

Today is your day to stir up your faith to receive your promise from My Word and press in to receive what Jesus has already paid the price with His Blood for you to receive.

Your part of walking in victory and overcoming your situation is to receive My promise by faith, praise Me like it is finished, and then enter into My peace, My rest, knowing that it will manifest in your life.

Be like the woman with the issue of blood. Settle in your heart that you are going to press in with your faith and take what already belongs to you.

Release your faith and acknowledge you have received your healing or your promise. It is the same faith to receive both. You using your faith is refreshing to Me, and it is releasing great power into your life.

Prayer – *Father, I come before You with a humble heart, and I thank You for the finished work of Jesus when He shed His Blood on the cross for me to be redeemed from the curse of the Law, sickness, lack, poverty, and disease. I am asking You to increase my faith to believe that I can receive not only my healing but everything my heart desires because I believe.*

Thoughts to Ponder.

Everywhere Jesus went, crowds of people followed Him. They wanted to see the miracles He performed. They were overjoyed to be in His presence, touching Him as they went. However, this one woman used her faith to press through the crowd to touch the tassel of His garment so she could lay hold of her promise of healing. What are you willing to do to receive your promise?

Taking Action To Grow Your Faith.

What is one thing from this verse that God is affirming to you right now regarding faith?

_____

_____

_____

After meditating on this verse, how does it inspire you to re-evaluate your faith journey?

_____

_____

_____

How will you apply this verse to your life so you can begin walking in even more faith to rise to a higher level of victory in your life?

_____

_____

_____

Day 27
The Testing Of Your Faith

My fellow believers, when it seems as though you are facing nothing but difficulties, see it as an invaluable opportunity to experience the greatest joy that you can! For you know that when your faith is tested it stirs up in you the power of endurance. James 1:2-3

My valued child, you are so precious to Me. You are my dearest treasure, and I cherish you. I understand that it seems as though you are facing nothing but difficult times right now. Your life looks as if there is one challenge coming fast on the heels of another without any reprieve.

Take a minute to breathe right now. Breathe in My love and goodness for you. Breathe in My peace and accept My grace. I want to assure you that as you experience each new trial, it is an invaluable occasion to trust Me even more. With each trial comes the opportunity for you to experience My great joy.

The trials you are encountering have come to test and prove your faith is strong and it is working to produce staying power or endurance. With each new trial, your faith helps you become more steadfast, and it produces more patience in your life.

As you allow endurance, steadfastness, and patience to grow even stronger in your life, your faith will release perfection into every part of your being until nothing is missing and nothing is lacking in your life. This is cause for great joy.

Prayer - *Father God, I come to You today humbly but boldly and confidently because of the Blood of Jesus. You have given me a new perspective on the many tests and trials I am encountering. So, today, I choose to count each test and trial as a blessing in my life. Thank You for reminding me that they produce endurance, patience, and steadfastness in my life.*

Thoughts to Ponder.

Choosing to look at your tests and trials from a heavenly perspective will help you have more joy in your life. When you realize the difficulties are producing endurance, steadfastness, and patience in your life, you can be certain your faith is releasing perfection into every part of your being until there is nothing missing and nothing lacking in your life.

Taking Action To Grow Your Faith.

What is one thing from this verse that God is affirming to you right now regarding faith?

_____

_____

_____

After meditating on this verse, how does it inspire you to re-evaluate your faith journey?

_____

_____

_____

How will you apply this verse to your life so you can begin walking in even more faith to rise to a higher level of victory in your life?

_____

_____

_____

Day 28
Your Faith Heals You

Jesus responded, "Your faith heals you. Go in peace, with your sight restored." All at once, the man's eyes opened and he could see again, and he began at once to follow Jesus, walking down the road with him. Mark 10:52

My esteemed child, as you sit in your affliction wondering how you will ever overcome it, be healed of it, or delivered from it, you can cry out to My Son, Jesus, right now just as blind Bartimaeus did when he knew Jesus was passing by him.

When Jesus heard Bartimaeus's cries for help, He recognized his persistent determination to get His attention. Bartimaeus knew if he could get to Jesus, he would receive his healing.

Although the disciples did not want Jesus to be bothered by Bartimaeus, Jesus sent his disciples to get Bartimaeus and bring him to Him. As Bartimaeus stood up and threw off his beggar's garment, he made his way to Jesus, knowing he would be healed.

Bartimaeus had the sound of faith in his voice that caught Jesus's attention. When Bartimaeus came to Jesus, Jesus said to him, "Go your way; your faith has healed you," and suddenly, Bartimaeus received his sight and went with Jesus.

Your faith has a sound that will produce results.

Prayer – *Father God, thank You for giving me faith that is demonstrated by my persistent determination to receive my healing. Thank You for giving me the revelation that faith is faith, and I can use my faith to receive everything I need from You. Thank You for recognizing my faith and honoring my faith. Thank You for showing me that my faith pleases You.*

Thoughts to Ponder.

Your faith has an action associated with it. Just as Bartimaeus displayed his faith by taking action to stand up and throw off his beggar's cloak, you can also change your position. You can make a stand with your faith by calling out to God through the Name of Jesus. God always honors your faith, and you will receive the desires of your heart through exercising your faith.

Taking Action To Grow Your Faith.

What is one thing from this verse that God is affirming to you right now regarding faith?

_____

_____

_____

After meditating on this verse, how does it inspire you to re-evaluate your faith journey?

_____

_____

_____

How will you apply this verse to your life so you can begin walking in even more faith to rise to a higher level of victory in your life?

_____

_____

_____

Day 29
A Heart Full Of Faith

I have fought an excellent fight. I have finished my full course with all my might and I've kept my heart full of faith. 2 Timothy 4:7

My awesome child, I urge you to be like Paul and live your life in such a way that whether the time is favorable for you, or it is not favorable, that you patiently correct and encourage people with good teachings and let your life be an example of how to live by faith.

Rise to the occasion whether it is convenient or not. Use the full expression of My Holy Spirit with wisdom and patience teaching people what is truth according to My Word.

The time is here when people no longer listen to and respond to the true healing words found in My Word because they are selfish and proud.

They look for teachers with soothing words that line up with their desires, only saying what they want to hear. They close their ears to the truth and believe the lies and myths.

It is time to be alert to these things and overcome every form of evil with My Word. Continue to carry the passion of your calling in your heart and fulfill the calling I have given you.

When you are ending your race, because of your life-long commitment, you will be able to say, 'I have fought an excellent fight. I have finished my full course with all my might, and I have kept my heart full of faith.'

Prayer – *Father God, as I come to You today, I thank You for giving me the strength to keep moving forward in the face of great opposition in season and out of season because my heart is full of faith. I ask You to give me wisdom by Your Holy Spirit, so I know the words of truth to speak to people so they can overcome every form of evil. I decree I am keeping the faith.*

Thoughts to Ponder.

The time has come when people no longer listen and respond to true instructions from the Word of God. Their itching ears long for something gratifying to satisfy their desires and foster errors they hold, causing them to wander off and reject the truth. However, you can keep a clear mind in every situation so you can confidently say you have kept a firm grip on your faith.

Taking Action To Grow Your Faith.

What is one thing from this verse that God is affirming to you right now regarding faith?

_____

_____

_____

After meditating on this verse, how does it inspire you to re-evaluate your faith journey?

_____

_____

_____

How will you apply this verse to your life so you can begin walking in even more faith to rise to a higher level of victory in your life?

_____

_____

_____

Day 30
Your Faith Is Your Victory Power

So fight with faith for the winner's prize! Lay your hands upon eternal life, to which you were called and about which you made the good confession before the multitude of witnesses! 1 Timothy 6:12

My adorable child, I created you, and you are invaluable to Me. My heart was filled with delight when I knit you together in your mother's womb.

If you have not already taken a hold of eternal life by believing in and confessing that My Son, Jesus, was buried and rose from death to life on the third day, I invite you to confess that now by faith so you will be with Me for eternity.

As my child, I call you to live your life in Holy awe, or reverential fear, of Me knowing I only have good plans for you. My desire is that you turn away from contention, competition, evil suspicions, and the love of money. Simply aim at and pursue righteousness, which is right standing with Me. Make it your goal to live a life of godliness which is the loving fear of Me and being Christlike. Fill your heart with faith, love, steadfastness, patience, gentleness, and tender humility.

Fight the good fight of the faith; do what you know to do with a clear conscience and without blemish until the appearance of your Lord Jesus Christ. This is your winner's prize.

Prayer – *Father God, thank You for sending Your Son, Jesus, to be the Savior of the world. I am using my faith to confess Him as my Savior and my Lord. I believe Jesus died and rose again from the dead, paying the ultimate price for me to have an intimate relationship with You. I decree I will live my life in Holy awe of You, focusing on fighting the good fight of faith.*

Thoughts to Ponder.

As God's child, He wants you to run away from the lusts and desires connected to this earthly kingdom that cause endless errors in your life. God desires you to chase after true holiness, justice, faithfulness, love, hope, patience, and tender humility. He knew you would need help in accomplishing these efforts, so He sent His Holy Spirit to be the Helper of your faith.

Taking Action To Grow Your Faith.

What is one thing from this verse that God is affirming to you right now regarding faith?

_____

_____

_____

After meditating on this verse, how does it inspire you to re-evaluate your faith journey?

_____

_____

_____

How will you apply this verse to your life so you can begin walking in even more faith to rise to a higher level of victory in your life?

_____

_____

_____

Prayer of Salvation

Pray this prayer to be born again and receive Jesus as your Lord and Savior.

Heavenly Father, I come to you in the Name of Jesus. Your Word says, *"If you openly declare that Jesus is Lord and believe in your heart that God raised him from the dead, you will be saved. For it is by believing in your heart that you are made right with God, and it is by openly declaring your faith that you are saved." Romans 10:9-10 NLT.*

I'm calling on You now, Jesus. I openly declare that Jesus is Lord, and I believe in my heart that God raised Him from the dead. It is that simple. You are now a born-again child of God.

The Bible says, *"If imperfect parents know how to lovingly take care of their children and give them what they need, how much more will the perfect heavenly Father give the Holy Spirit's fullness when his children ask him." Luke 11:13.*

I'm asking You to fill me with the Holy Spirit. Holy Spirit, rise up within me as I praise God. I expect to speak with other tongues as You give me utterance according to Acts 2:4, which says, *"They were all filled and equipped with the Holy Spirit and were inspired to speak in tongues—empowered by the Spirit to speak in languages they had never learned!"*

Now, worship and praise God as you are filled with the Holy Spirit and speak in your heavenly language, your first language, or other tongues.

About Lucia M. Claborn

Lucia Claborn is a victory coach, author, and speaker. She helps people who have been hurt by church or life find restoration by building their faith to discover their true identity, so they can walk in victory.

Her heartbeat is to teach people to stand on the Word of God, decree and declare their desired world into existence, and release their faith to receive their heart's desires.

Lucia has been writing for more than 30 years, with her recent books being available on Amazon as well as countless publishing platforms around the world.

Her weekly podcast, Secrets to Victorious Living, encourages listeners around the world by building their faith to walk in victory.

Lucia and her husband, Danny, live in North Alabama. They have four grown children and four grandchildren. You can find Lucia online at:

LuciaClaborn.com
Facebook: LuciaMClaborn
Instagram: @Lucia.Claborn
Clubhouse: Lucia Claborn - Celebrating Victorious Living

Other Products Available From
Lucia M. Claborn

Books
English Version
ABC's Of Who I Am - Decreeing Who God Says I Am
ABC's Of Who I Am Journal - Decreeing Who God Says I Am
Your Victory In The Making – A 30-Day Devotional
Your Power & Authority In The Making – A 30-Day Devotional
Faith Builders For Victorious Living, Decree Your Victory – A 365-Day Devotional

Spanish Version
ABC's De Quien Soy – Decretando Quién Dice Dios Que Soy Yo
ABC's De Quien Soy Diario – Decretando Quién Dice Dios Que Soy
En Vísperas de Tu Victoria – Un Devocional de 30 Días

Podcast
Secrets to Victorious Living
Listen On Stitcher, iTunes or
your favorite podcast platform.

www.ingramcontent.com/pod-product-compliance
Lightning Source LLC
Chambersburg PA
CBHW060350130626
46553CB00003B/1168